The Terms of His Surrender

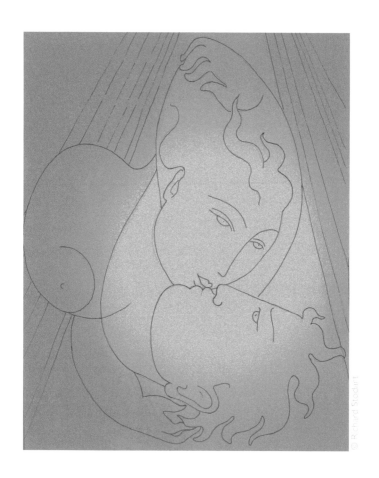

The Terms of His Surrender

David John Schleich

Richard Stodart, Illustrator

Crusoe House
USA: Portland, Oregon
Canada: Vancouver, British Columbia

Text and cover design,
cover art and frontispiece by Richard Stodart

Some poems in this collection appeared in earlier versions
in *All the Messiahs Agree*, 2017, now out of print.

ISBN: 978-0-9996233-2-9 hardcover
ISBN: 978-0-9996233-3-6 epub
Library of Congress Control Number: 2021912721

Printed in the United States of America

Crusoe House
USA: Portland, Oregon
Canada: Vancouver, BC
crusoehouse@gmail.com

contents

If love wants you;
if you've been melted down to stars,
you will love with lungs and gills;
with feathers and scales;
with warm blood and cold.

anne michaels

I love you as the plant that never blooms
but carries in itself the light of hidden flowers;
thanks to your love a certain solid fragrance
risen from the earth, lives darkly in my body

pablo neruda

Trust your heart if the seas catch fire,
live love though the stars walk backward.

e.e. cummings

the ache of men

she finds him lingering
where the sea licks the sand
she coaxes his soul to higher ground
where already she has staked a place
to evoke in them without apology
what rare rain stirs in brown desert

that she found him on this vast littoral
accumulates as dense mystery
dares disturb the universe
they leave no scar at all

no small matter how miraculous her form
exactly how he loves the feminine

they understand as one clenched soul
this geography of tense and person

dune woman

she is walking north through sedge and sweet gale
in search of him this day
headed to bare sand hummocks
bounded by morning glory

her head is down, against the spray
her quick feet crush culm as she sweeps
past flat-floored blowouts
and beachheads of new grass

she finds him canted by an ancient ventifact
watching long grey waves pulsing in
each swash disturbing mirror bits of tiny suns
setting fire to testimonies of the unrequited

the air he breathes he knows is also breathed by her
their holy forms brace against the sea
the wind stings their eyes
and their endless looking

he loves, she loves
it is enough they are right there
they can hear the ocean
doing what it does

the recognition

they happen on a language billowing and familiar
from that moment they memorize every word
that tastes of hearts on fire

they embed their own Esperanto
into riprap against the dinning scour
for they know no matter what its name is
it is love that is not sinning

all night her name is smooth riffing
its shape round and letters lavender
its sound sloping to the diminutive
her perfect lips are wordless
breathing into him the memory of touch
spring warm seducing every splintered puddle
in their way

the idea of the other snaps open
touched to the core they are
by the first breath grabbing kiss
and entering heat

persisting winter, bark-rough
does not slow the unravelling ice and white
the casting out of cold bloated facts
long locked and tough

probable canvas

one swipe of her blue eyes
snags his malaise
she flings it over her shoulder
dowsing every heresy behind them

you are the last of your kind, she says
for some feelings are reached
only through poetry
or skin on skin

the delicate green faces of humming birds
are stitched into hoops of fiddler's cloth, two over two
his heart disappears like an old idea
into the flapping sleeves of their day

every sonnet in him shuts tight
until the idea of her is taut
like a probable canvas

ritual truth

he lays his cheek against her bare shoulder
continuing their ritual truth
she insinuates the cold arches of her small feet
into the soft warm curves behind his knee
searching for a night's berth
his legs are a grave
her lips are soft spades

making for the temple

deep in verdant woods
lured from hidden lairs back in
a big cat watches hunter green vines circle their legs
witnesses ancient conundrums begin

the lovers shed city vestments
pad quickly through the friable understory
making for the temple

the cat's eyes narrow
to study every fluid move
recede and follow
they are all new pilgrims

sheltering before waking

a great ocean rain from the west blows in
soaking the coastal path
they turn east where thick mist beckons
with rumours of inland forest shelter

they rest on mounds of feuilles mortes
honeyed old gold leaves
atop mossy philomot understory

anon they find fresh fur remnants and ancient growth
left by absent tan fox squirrels and cream gray chipmunks
who screamed once in this place
and left the scent of menace and terror both

the earth below has waited centuries
to reformulate
pushes up and out under the recent green canopy
detonates any memory of visitors

impending splendid green

not once did his heart hesitate to meet
the strength of her arms
pulling him away from the queue of witnesses
who mime bland secrets on every street

he obeys the dangerous new code of touch
trembles below this tower of a new order
for they had thought they could not love again
suddenly, weeks of love in hours

at dawn he implores the world for redemption
to save him from her beauty
and when later he asks
about the new ballad of their bodies
their desire descends momentarily to grief

she weeps behind her veil
for what is true and strange
for the good of this love

they trace the answer between them
their fingers arcing, hers, his
touching brave, tiny benediction blue lungwort
and he remembers again the fragile power
of impending splendid green

just out of reach

the imprint of her touch coils
covers his body with pools of her
they are two dancers floating
settling like bones on ancient soil

her hands are kiss tipped arrows
whose elegant fletchings steer
murmurs of their fenced passion
to the same mark every new morning
though they blur as they near

still, he knows what makes him man
her eyes, her kiss, her tears
he knows the whole strength of her body
braced and locked all over him

a red bird blissed on spring
threads its throwaway path
demonstrating for each
forbidden morning lineaments
just out of reach

holding hands in broad daylight

in their joy, in their fire
they hold hands at Wolf Point
stop on the Riverwalk a while
to catalogue the other's beauty

he traces his heart on the pad of her palm
attracting the attention of strangers who know them
he announces how well he understands
the advance of her breasts beneath his hands
testifying they are no longer neglected

and for the record, another adds
that the thighs of the bride
are awake and burning
now that the war is on

they scale every wall of the city streets
and watch themselves from the other side
everyone wants what they have
holding hands in broad daylight

for what counts tonight
is how near they sleep
ignoring every searchlight

later they lie temporarily in ruins
and study silently the wake of the tether
which ties their vow not to suffer
to their very communion

the grace of lovers

the grace of lovers slides up his spine tonight
so weary at three a.m. is he
recalling how her voice coaxed song birds
from their cotes in spring just gone

she filled the air with butterflies
her flicking fingers and swerving palms
danced an absent essence
filling his room with Babylon

he rises, goes deeper into the sanctuary
where crows assembled earlier to deliberate
he finds there the peace of creatures
who never hesitate, their forethought always instant

she, like Sirius and the Centauries
is not there above this lair
absent travelling images all
he hears her nonetheless
life is not done with us by far, she is saying
and then the raw scream of the last late crow
rips the sky's greying caul again

all the messiahs agree

each time his hand feels her absence on the bed
he could not love her beryl eyes the more
nor when he looks up from her panting gut
and listens to their breathing

all the Messiahs agree
their lips sip desire like hummingbirds
he kisses her open mouth
while they lie on the plain bed
eating all the cake he brought
for the celebration

later it rains and guardian angels appear
washing them clean
reminding them to put away anything
which can comfort the enemy camp

he asks her to dance
under the blurred halo of the alley lamp
she asks him to grow spring wings with her
and lose their minds

instead they stay and read Karenina
he whispers the birthday song he wrote
and for a moment the verses change the skies
but then their minds pour poison which they drink
lassoing their naked arms, closing down their eyes

they send back to the sun
the spring buds of future flowers
and tell each other their histories
they give their hearts outright
to silence the eidolons an hour

like improvident tapers in blue wind
they wait for the times to change
until elusive taunts hiss from outside the pane
where water has collected on the ledge
they have refrained from using yet
to put out the fire in them

the sulphur priest

they go together to the temple
where benedictions are mysterious
and indulgences of the Raccolta severe
for those who cannot breathe

for want of absolution
the clergy rings the moisture from her
they lash his back for thirsting
condemn them to a far away pillory

behind the temple curtain
duty priests in linen words chant their conviction
you lingered too long on her thighs
she moved you like some feral vixen

the sinners' heads bow before them
and in the darkened chancel
the witnesses barely hear him say
she is an angel from far Babylon
no other ever touched me so

the sulphur priest flicks lit lunts at them
sets fire their rose-cheeked beauty
splays their waists on the pinning block

every temple, every sacristy decrees
they shall be formless now
scorned and absent from the other

lured by secret sulphur signals
from inside the dark confessional others kneel
mourning quietly

when they lie down

she looks up with eyes that are morning sun
they both are new inside her
her smile pulls his essence unutterably in
just as the sea embraces every lonely sailor

he reels in this falling
the heads of lovers on every continent turn in unison
to look and learn this love
whole forests are pulled skyward
like rising flocks of doves

he is eager for this sacred duty
his arms sheathe the tyranny of her beauty
and when his shoulders drop to her
he claims the change from both to one
and they are cured by their learning
an eimi of two, no longer in fear of fallen saints

they possess the soft eyes of satyrid butterflies
weary from flight
but the mercy of their prayer is angelic
their exiled selves infinite and precise

the terms of his surrender

on the last day he knelt to confess
the terms of his surrender
wept privately, not wanting to offend her

guardian angels overheard him
can we dance once more, he asked
before you go, before we have to go

whence the intimate mercy of your lips
he whispered the question urgently
he pleaded to live beside her

but her case was packed, concluded
I have loved you all the cruel spring long, she said
and look, we have come through, instead

he cannot breathe without her
the mark her breasts made on him
will remain a sin til morning
when he will beg all lovers of the world to forgive them
guided by signals in their skin

the keepers of the garden of beloveds
carry off their bodies prone and bare
they tie signs around their necks
he forgets to ask for a lock of her hair

sad proscenium

his hands square a proscenium
of forest and fast river
she moves into the frame
beckoned by the blurred bank opposite
where a little one watches
mama, I'm here
the tiny whisper joining all their words
already set free on the water
skitting the riffles like whirligig beetles

she does not hesitate
bends, pulls the water in around her
swims headlong again
toward the moment of birth
every pull of her arms and slash of her legs
making for the farther shore

in the trees above
another figure gestures weakly

the name of the beloved

she heard her name announced
at the airports of foreign countries
she slid segments of Fuyu persimmons
slowly into her mouth
sitting on the boulevard of their Paris café

he invited her to watch from a balcony in Barcelona
where they stood above the scurrying relics and lances
of the crusaders on the Rambla Catalunya
he put his arms around her from behind
and spoke their will into her hair
she turned and kissed everything
she had missed before

then her name flew
like the unlimited grey moon out to sea
like a blue cotton dress caught in a gust
she sidled her back into his breath and his alone
it mattered not a wit what the witnesses made of that

today he died

she arrived at the porous ceremony
her eulogy announced that his body was done
she beckoned the mourning angels in the aisles
she implored morning light sneaking out in front of stars
she asked the fish finning downstream
when is it ever as easy as that
a dying and a forgetting

there came as well to hear her speak
a shadow man arriving at the wake
a heart beating red in his dripping pack

when she left, his soul followed furtively
pushing aside the water and the light in their way
both healing behind the intrusion
an elegance of slow eternal refolding

alert as an officer on the field of fire
his dead eyes fastened on her
they remembered at once the holiness of their happiness

there is nothing more mysterious, he said
than dying on this pained precipice
this hot pyre where love prevails imperially
and softens the carnage around the magistrates
who report all such warmth warm as unknowable

every perfect single flake of late snow

passed slowly and without protest
upon the warming earth of spring

testament in rock

they returned to their place under the pine canopy
where footprints of lovers endure
she heard him say as they lay there
god let me let you in

he knew that pilgrims with small brushes centuries hence
would brush up traces of the frankincense they breathed
left behind by scraping ice
he prayed too for shoots of love to shoulder up
from smothered dull roots
escaping veins of truth running close to the bone
testament of love locked down
hushed seductive and dangerous
like slow magma

as softly as the weightless passing butterfly
which alighted on their rock
they clasped love against their chests
so wounded were they then

that no one could hurt them more

again

eggs in a nest

he was talking to her in his solitude
and singularity
his heart as hard as flint that day
until he came upon an untended nest
eggs oddly olive there in the lesser celandine
marked in squiggles of brown and black

like the fearful monk reflecting on the chalice
which Tristan and Isolde did not refuse
and a kingdom wobbled into war thereby
he tried whistling
and startled two terns from the sea
pale grey and white below
who swooped and ascended rapidly
to and from the forest floor

failed watcher of their flight
he missed the detail of their wings
and the lesson of their wandering

the perfect courtesy of water

the usual tricks no longer work
his whole life smaller now
a mess by every measure
exhausted arms can not hold it all
like the perfect courtesy of water
love lets her in

she closes around his soul
then she says with religious attention
the sea will heave, the earth undulate
making and unmaking
the immutable sky

mad love will tend our purposes
the hands of love around our throats
without apology

she looks at him, past him
remembering like a knife blade
that spring in the pinewood

fleeing to Catalonia

her absence is a fist in his belly
the untameable becomes foreboding
an alliance of the condemned for his cell

he moves in on the bruising
kicks out the racket of it
banishes the nameless place in his body
where the weight of her lives

he aches to nuzzle every part
to see her seeing him
blades moving like the ouroboros
hem her endlessly in and away from him
gone, gone her breath all night in the dark

burrow, dissimulate
do whatever it takes, he cries
pass a week in Barcelona with me
I'll get your ticket, buy red wine for you
we'll stay awake all the day long
the heaven of touch will see us through

barcarole in six/eight time

he imagines her alone on a balcony at the Bauer-Grunwald
lifting a wineglass
plucking at the memory of her beryl eyes there in Venice
wafting notes in murmurations
which feint away from them

her waist is the place where chords gather behind strings
the cusp where misformed notes can go
blending with the crumbled swirl of moist kissing

the melody of love was at once warm rain
succumbing to gravity
they become a stream
yearning for the same sea all lovers know

he is a gondolier on the Grand Canal
in the shadow of Santa Maria della Salute
mouthing his barcarole in six/eight time
rowing to her in the dark
weeping in his strength and his weakness
the memory of touch shutting out the stubborn empty place
where this flat bottomed boat meets the water

making for the beginning

while masons work on the walls
of their decaying homes
they go to their table in their café by the sea
to allay the slow fade they fled
cirrus love inside a lie
they make for Catalonia

a church bell on Sunday morning
awakens them in the Pulitzer
their bodies issue reports
of desire sliding into grief

they flee to the desert
and in the shade of dark terebinths
compose sad songs about all they live without
about wet red silk on skin
about their particularity

on their way to receive the Holy Spirit
they dare not look back
at the salt lovers they pass

when time runs out
they make for the beginning
but find their table taken
and the sea deeper
colder
brimming

the longing has no proprietor

leaning at night in the Cathedral door
he writes her down like a photograph
he is a grey chalice heaped tall
with those days and nights
when they feared say their names at all

she looked at him for so long
that he stepped behind her eyes
to look out at their exiled bodies
and ask what became of them

he saw around her neck like a noose
the resplendent red bandana they used
to wipe back tears of unknown origin

he went far and high
to chant her privately in his vespers
unable to disguise the secret love between them
from the watching crowd

he went regularly to Paris
to live their fantasy
her legs around his body
her eyes inside of him

their bodies were not yet cleansed by banishment
stooping them to sad strategies
soft facts and fractions frothed up immutable

each one just in this moment
roving sorrows
incomplete, inscrutable

somber honey

making endings lays him low
causes him to hold his breath too long
somber honey playing this trick on them both
propagating dull strikes on this particular spot

there was a time when writing her name
excited untrimmable mornings
now the sound stored under his tongue
startles when it erupts
and the witnesses who eschew such frumious lament
banish him to room after room
where an empty chair broods in each

frame of mind

sweet leafy stalks are indifferent to the brisk breeze
which whips her hair about a bit
and somewhere near the kerfuffle
scuts of quick small critters go about their business
bending fast past the tree with red berries
a meadow rowan as confident as old oak
who's seen it all, or a lot at least
whose sibling black flexuous rods sometimes face a
different fate
rustic, even brash a while on this hill

and where this stalky living burst emerges from the earth
oyster grass is its companion
never so firm, never so tall
smooth cordgrass prospering briefly on top
underneath, dense roots making a marsh of it all
their dead stalks washing soon to the sea
to feed tiny beings at the bottom

while up here on the shore there is a hut
whose walls long for her

the petrel and the fletcher

they dispatched the ancient petrel far to sea
climb fast and high and then descend again, they said
hover as you do above us
circle in the night
one day you will be our beacon
our compass, in high familiar flight

when your vigil is complete
and we are bidden back to cross the grimpen mire
carry we will our hidden love
and the wisdom of the fire
the sonnet in us waiting like a promise
to protect clenched love in spaces treacherous

like taxing stones in a river
there are those who may slow us
or refuse to let us pass
but spring love aimed true by the feathers
of an arrow from the mythic fletcher's quiver
will course fearless over all of that
for are we not conspirators?
is enchantment not our future?

though new witnesses may eschew the petrel's flight
or love as never sin
they will see by our eyes
however vexed to silence we were then

our flesh, our hearts now prove otherwise
meaning, she said to him in endless answering
only now, only you

all I live without

the goddess makes the sea endlessly answer
roll in again, ferret out words sunk
by undulations not of her making

she buries the ones he never thought to speak
carves them elsewhere into soaked littoral
her spilling waves obscure where she has been hiding
her lips are printed deftly on the clay cup
he abandoned in the sand for her to find

he watches her pulled back by the swash
as the sea reach does what it must
solving every river's yearning

she promises to return with a cargo of roses
to atone for endless sculpting and leaving
her random caresses slowing always, though
behind the swells

lovers at the chilled shore

he comes to the nameless shore
to watch white gannets explode deep into grey water
the birds blaze down deep
scattering schools who were curious

his once scarlet love is scumbled now
like old fire and blood, more nothing than something
syllables tighten which once sprang full
from both their mouths

his eyes are squeezed shut
the longing less that way
the sweet good of it all out there somewhere

he washes his eyes in the salt sea
he thinks he sees her
just where the steel grey water laves the shore's chilled sand
and surrounds his feet

he's sure a curlew wails just to him
and to frightened watchers

on the dark green hill

light travels easily in spring
over the dark green hill
where listening is lonely

an ambling brown cow
its washy trail a sure sign of early pasturing
can't get a mouthful first try
the sweet gold bottom stems stay
promising tall fescue, bunchgrass and foxtail
each sheath and blade a miracle

when next he comes to this hill
to lie lost in green and brown
he will try again the trick of whistling grass
tearing the thick end of one, a single one
and squeezing shut the other

spring grazing took too much water from this flat green thing
its weak walls won't make the sound he wants
so the tips of a thousand blades are now boats in an armada
an inflorescence of dense panicle hats, yellow and green
stepping lightly and lazily into a boy's private army

the sneers of boys and old men

unearned sneers of boys and old men
are bile talk of love
claiming their bodies flag by flag
and like an advancing conqueror
weaving and unweaving weight onto their legs

still they move on forest paths north of the city
the careful pace of staccato scouts
showing the way

he wants her hands on his temples
to help them dissolve their Faustian love
on its tumbly legs

and now there is spring
pronouncing her green name again
the slow prayer of water fretting
down to the sea
spilling over smooth stones which worry the flow

the stone-hard descent of hearts breaking
cascades through a chute in the way

scavenger

she sent him away with a checklist:
any rock, a black rock, a bug, a red bug with wings
an inscribed photograph, an egg

he comes back sooner than expected
because he remembers the green shirt she left behind
ten years before, the night she woke at dawn
and fled ahead of the threat of first morning words

identification and possession are your mission, she said
these leaves, twigs, berries, and the egg don't cut it
don't forget the aleph, she added
a branch, simply, with two little twigs attached

kindling

inside a patch of woolly mullein
he has built a grass bunker

from here a meadowlark's bell chupp just outside
he can see her weaving her domed nest
in a hollow of their same earth

inside he is on fire
crackling like transforming kindling
in a grate blue hot soon black
the staccato note of her calling
is no soft rattle

for he knows she is fleeing

the health of my soul

he was sixteen
a girl in blue culottes, arms akimbo
eschewed his smile as they passed on a path
betrayed with spangling eyes what she knew full well
was beguilement

now he is an old man
remembering that great defeat
knowing just ahead waits another one
to awaken him from long revery
in which trees frame the lane he fled down
to run off her blue eyed shun

later in tall grass he lay a while
where some fell clutch of resignation stitched him to the earth
but above a kingfisher assembled into a dive
its crown and neck slipped into his closed eyes
a shot of blue neither sky nor her
pinched his ears with a rattling squall
her undulant unbroken arc carved right through
his malaise

the bird and the bird sharing the air
still ornament his mind today with gratitude

on the way back he crossed the neighbour's field
where a Percheron with no plough to pull
came right up to him, velvet nostrils wet, flared and full

she breathed him in, backed away
he leaned into her to listen, but she turned
and he heard the whisk of that elegant tail

near cold fear

1

in black chasuble the priest prays over them
he is ripe with folly, the spoils of simony
under his red stole and white cincture

2

to the arriving column he shouts out goals
one more hill, one valley more, my sons
the last sacrament assured for every soul
promises too that the Tigris, Euphrates, Pishon and Gihon
will assemble a new convergence
just for them

3

but they know this darksome delta burn
of rogue weeds, silt and wildness
they know its crafty serpent's rattle
for they are armed pilgrims shuffling
into the valley neck of battle
where every old and best command
crowds their ears and cracks their veins

4

once again they are comforted
by an assembly of the saved
who gather for the fresh apocalypse

though their souls are stained
by the sin of near cold fear

5

the river just ahead falls inexorably
into cold nahash-brimming sea
and around them like courtiers
all the devils agree
that the priest need not explain
the fleeing idea of black

6

their tails stick out like comic beacons
of an old idea
their horns grow inwards
to the centre of a dark understanding

7

from the hills tranced syndics speculate
and in their savvy, order every officer
to concede the rout, its outcomes so familiar
and to wipe all blood from the backs of their hands

8

for they are peddlers who tally incessantly
document the trait and trace of every sortie
while indifferent gods nearby await their sums
and stay busy binding desire in eloquent caution
dismissing every called for comity

9

from their graveled verge old men and women cry
I was once your father and your mother
and now, prisoners all
we march in brief right angles

10

later when the battle subsides to silence
there come many maidens crying
'Do not die; I love you so'
but still they keep on dying

about the author

David Schleich is the former publisher and editor of Quarry Press and *Quarry Magazine*. He is a retired university president and widely published essayist and columnist. He frequently presents in the health and higher education fields.